MW01088608

HowExpert Guide to High School Cross Country Coaching

How to Coach High School Cross Country From A to Z

HowExpert with Kyle Daubs

Copyright HowExpert™
www.HowExpert.com

For more tips related to this topic, visit
HowExpert.com/crosscountrycoaching.

Recommended Resources

- HowExpert.com – Quick 'How To' Guides on All Topics from A to Z by Everyday Experts.
- HowExpert.com/free – Free HowExpert Email Newsletter.
- HowExpert.com/books – HowExpert Books
- HowExpert.com/courses – HowExpert Courses
- HowExpert.com/clothing – HowExpert Clothing
- HowExpert.com/membership – HowExpert Membership Site
- HowExpert.com/affiliates – HowExpert Affiliate Program
- HowExpert.com/writers – Write About Your #1 Passion/Knowledge/Expertise & Become a HowExpert Author.
- HowExpert.com/resources – Additional HowExpert Recommended Resources
- YouTube.com/HowExpert – Subscribe to HowExpert YouTube.
- Instagram.com/HowExpert – Follow HowExpert on Instagram.
- Facebook.com/HowExpert – Follow HowExpert on Facebook.

From the Publisher

Dear HowExpert reader,

HowExpert publishes quick 'how to' guides on all topics from A to Z by everyday experts.

At HowExpert, our mission is to discover, empower, and maximize talents of everyday people to ultimately make a positive impact in the world for all topics from A to Z...one everyday expert at a time!

All of our HowExpert guides are written by everyday people just like you and me who have a passion, knowledge, and expertise for a specific topic.

We take great pride in selecting everyday experts who have a passion, great writing skills, and knowledge about a topic that they love to be able to teach you about the topic you are also passionate about and eager to learn about.

We hope you get a lot of value from our HowExpert guides and it can make a positive impact in your life in some kind of way. All of our readers including you altogether help us continue living our mission of making a positive impact in the world for all spheres of influences from A to Z.

If you enjoyed one of our HowExpert guides, then please take a moment to send us your feedback from wherever you got this book.

Thank you and we wish you all the best in all aspects of life.

Sincerely,

BJ Min
Founder & Publisher of HowExpert
HowExpert.com

PS...If you are also interested in becoming a HowExpert author, then please visit our website at HowExpert.com/writers. Thank you & again, all the best!

Table of Contents

Introduction

At the young age of 23, I started a cross country program for the small high schools of Lowpoint-Washburn and Roanoke-Benson. At the age of 26, I have been very blessed to learn from my mistakes and progress as a cross country coach. It is my belief that some of the best to ever do anything are the ones that have to learn on their own.

I was never able to run cross country in high school. I was a two-time conference champion in junior high in the 1600 meter run, but never stepped foot on a track for Charleston High School. At age 14, I had some stomach problems that were never diagnosed. I lost 40 pounds and my body could not keep food down. I could not participate in sports for three years. I weighed 120 pounds at the end of my junior year.

I eventually healed up and was able to play sports my senior year, and after that I got back into running. I am a self-made runner that has trained for years. I have run three marathons, 15 half marathons, and dozens of 10Ks and 5Ks.

What I am trying to say is that this book will not feed you information from a coach that has been in the game for half a century like the great Joe Newton. This book will give readers a younger coach's perspective of what it takes to succeed. In this book, I will explain to the best of my ability what has worked for my program, so that other first time coaches can blossom. Maybe, older coaches who are looking to evolve will learn something new too.

I coach for a co-op that has a combined 300 school enrollment. I am lucky to get 10 boys and 10 girls for a season. My last three years, I have averaged 9 boys and 8 girls. Some of these practices are best suited for a small school environment,

I have learned a lot, and I still have a lot to learn. I have not even reached half a decade of coaching yet, but I would like to share with you what I have learned through my trial and error. I want to share with you what I have learned from my mentors that have helped guide me. I hope that this book will help you grow too. Let's get at it.

Kyle Daubs

Chapter 1: Communicating Your Coaching Philosophy

This opening chapter will show you how to develop a coaching philosophy, how to set goals, and how to communicate that to your team. Cross country season is typically during the fall months of August to October for schools in Illinois. However, if an athlete wants to develop, the season is year round with a few breaks thrown here and there.

Develop A Philosophy

There's an old quote out there. It goes, "if you love what you do, it ain't working." That goes for your job, but especially coaching. Have you ever noticed that losing teams always look like they have no interest in being where they are? Cross country is different when it comes to overall team records as more of the focus can be on the individual's improvement. However, you need individual improvement, so that the team can improve as well.

That improvement will come when athletes are being pushed by a coach that wants to be there. As a coach, you have to love the job and the kids. The kids will follow the example that you lead.

When you are developing your philosophy, be prepared for it to change. My first year coaching, my focus was more on the improvement of the times of the runners. We were a bunch of rag tag athletes, who were not ready to compete. After my second season, I preached winning conferences and making the Sectional. By my third year, we thought we could win a few invites, and we did.

You need to have rules. You are the boss of your team, but there is nothing wrong with formulating a rapport either. Be stern, but be caring. Push the kid to their max potential, but still care about what goes on in their life. A kid will only do so much based on their respect level for you in my opinion.

Developing Rules

I keep my rules simple. I also keep them in broad terms to where they can umbrella other minor rules.

1. Show up to practice: You only get three unexcused absences. I believe in three strikes, you are out.
2. Show up on time: If the bus leaves at 7:00, you show up at 6:55. If you show up at 7:01, we have left.
3. You cheer for your family: This sport is hard, but it is easier when you have a family supporting you. When the girls race, the boys support the girls. When the boys race, the girls support the boys. It goes the same for practices.
4. Filtering: I have said a few "bad words" at practice. At practice, we talk about how we talk with our family and friends. I tell parents about

the language, so they are aware. However, when we are in public, we filter our language. That's a life skill for them to develop.

5. Team gear: Finally, we wear our team shirts to school before or on the day of a meet. We wear our sweats together. We are a team. We are in unison.

Keeping The Team Communicating

In a team sport, you do not work alone. You must communicate your knowledge and approach to your team, coaches, and parents. You will never coach a team where you do not talk to someone through speaking or writing.

When you develop a philosophy, you have planned the culture of your team. How can you communicate that to the team? The hope is that you are not alone. You will hopefully have assistant coaches. You will have your school administration. You will have parents, the community, and media.

Communicating With Athletes

The first, and most important, group of people you want to be communicating are your team. When your team buys into your approach, the message will spread like wildfire. The team is a group of athletes.

You will have to establish communication with your athletes. There are two main things that I do at each practice, so that each athlete feels valued.

First, I have daily announcements before the kids warm up. I call out each kid's name, so that they know that I know they are here. When the coach acknowledges who is here it does not make the athlete feel they are a ghost.

Second, I make sure to have a conversation at least one time with each athlete at each practice. I want the athletes to know that I care if they are there. For larger teams, you can have each kid "check out" with you before they leave. That way you do not leave anyone out.

I am really big into nicknames. I feel that when you give nicknames it creates a special bond. The nickname does not have to be super creative. It can be as simple as some of these: Vic (Victoria), Lou (Lucy), A-Aron (Aaron), etc.

In the end, it is your job to communicate with your athletes. You need to get them to buy into your message. Not just the captains either. Everyone on the team needs to feel valued. By making them feel important, they are more likely to buy what you are selling.

Communicating With The Team

Team meetings are necessary. I briefly mentioned that we have announcements before stretching in the last section. These meetings are used for telling athletes about upcoming meets, recognition of personal bests, eligibility and grades in the classroom, and the workout for the day.

I never tell kids what the workout will be until practice. If we have harder workouts, the athletes will come to practice with a sour attitude because it is "harder." Plus, school comes first. They need to perform in the classroom, so that they can run cross country. They do not need to be thinking about practice at that given moment.

Private Communication

There will be times that you will not be happy with members of your team. That could have something to do with their performance in a meet, practice, or attitude. There are other ways to address these issues.

I am different from other coaches. I allow the athletes to have access to my cell phone. I suffer from depression, so I tell my athletes if there is ever a time to talk, they can text me, or call me if needed. My door is always open if I am not there face to face.

I use texting if athletes are down on themselves and need to talk. Most of the time these conversations happen in the evening. I typically do not talk to athletes if it is very late in the evening, but I have had a few occurrences where sometimes they needed to just vent about something else going on in their lives.

I do not text athletes every day. I let them come to me. Most of the time, an athlete and I will talk through texting twice during the season. However, this is not the case for everyone.

If I have an issue with performance, I rather talk to my athletes face to face. Sometimes in texting, what you say can be taken the wrong way. Face to face, I know what I am saying and how I am saying it.

The best way to talk in private is to address what you are upset about. Do not come off as attacking and never be demeaning. You are a coach. You criticize for improvement, but never to bring someone down. I always let the athlete voice their concerns and ask for their opinion. Communication is a two way street, so I care what they have to say.

A lot of coaches go the drill sergeant path. I find that unsuccessful. This is a sport, not boot camp. If they wanted to be in the military, they would have joined military school.

Using Social Media To Promote

For the team, I created a Facebook group. At our parents meeting, I invite all parents and athletes to the group. Over the years, alumni stay in the group, so our page has grown. I usually let the parents invite the other parents because it makes them feel involved. Plus, most of the parents know each other and I am not friends with them on social media.

I also use an app called Remind. I have all parents give me their cell phone number, so I can send updates or snapshots of the cross country invites. This app will send one message to all numbers at the same time, so it saves a lot of time compared to communicating with each parent.

I like to use both of these apps because some parents do not have Facebook, so they can receive updates through messaging. I really love the Facebook group because that is where I can post results immediately after the meet is over. Not all parents can make meets, but they still want to know how their child performed.

By using social media, you are keeping everyone informed. When the parent knows how their child performs, they can give them praise when they get home. Plus, I post personal bests. For the parents who are very involved, they will congratulate other members on the team who are not their kids. That makes the athletes feel special and it builds self confidence.

Keeping Assistant Coaches Involved

My first year coaching I had no assistant. I also had to practice at two different schools. I would practice at one school, while the athletes at the other school would practice on the "honor code." It was not ideal because I was doing everything on my own.

The last two years, I have had an assistant coach. It has been a godsend having her around. She takes care of a lot of the behind the scenes stuff. Plus, some of the athletes connect with her better than me. That does not bother me at all. I am just glad our athletes feel connected by someone.

Your assistant coach needs to have a role. I communicate with my assistant coach daily during the season. I send her practice plans during the day, so that she knows what is happening. I also tell her what each of us will be doing.

For days that we have recovery runs, it is a little bit more chill. However, when we have speed workouts, it is nice having multiple timers, so we can have multiple groups go.

Your assistant coach is there to help the athletes progress as runners. They are also there to give you feedback. I always tell my assistant coach to give me input. I am an emotional coach, and sometimes I react. She is calm, and will tell me how I should go about a problem sometimes, which I appreciate. You as the head coach have the final say, but sometimes it is nice having another perspective.

Communicating With The Media

For this section, I am including the school. When you are successful, you should let the rest of the school know. I always make sure to give the school highlights of our results, so they can include them in their announcements. When other members of the school see that you are successful, they might want to join your program.

The media can include your newspaper. We are the smallest school in our area, so getting press coverage is hard except for when we go to conference or the postseason. The coverage does not come automatic.

I will email with reporters when something special happens. For example, one of our girls broke the school record, so I emailed the reporter. The media in our area has nearly 40 schools to cover, so it is impossible to think they are going to know everything that happens at your school. The coaches make the coverage happen.

Chapter 2: The Keys to Motivating in High School Cross Country

Motivating starts with the coach. The coach shares the dream, makes a plan how to get you there, and builds competitiveness among his/her team. Motivation is hard in general. Think about your own goals. Have you accomplished everything you wanted even when it gets hard?

The motivation to run well has to come from the individual, team, and the coach who leads the charge. In this section, I will summarize some of the best motivation tactics that I have deemed successful for my team.

Motivating The Runners By S.M.A.R.T. Goals

The very first part of business I do at the beginning of the year is I preach my goals for the team. Typically, my team goals are winning conferences and making the sectional. However, I require everyone to set an individual goal and a team goal.

The goals need to be S.M.A.R.T. That means the goal needs to be specific, measurable, attainable, realistic, and timely. Sometimes, an athlete will need a goal modified. If you have an athlete that sets an individual goal of running a 21:00 three mile, but ran a 9:00 minute mile time trial. In order to set a new goal, you need to communicate with the athlete.

You should not make a new goal for the athlete. You as the coach should offer advice and make a new goal that the athlete will feel comfortable with. For this particular athlete above, setting a goal of a 26-minute three mile would be a good start. Nine minute mile pace would be a 27:00 three mile. Explain to the athlete to hit this goal, and then you can evaluate a new goal.

That is what is great about cross country. I always set new goals for the athletes. I had an athlete set a goal to run a 25:00 three mile, but ran a 23:32 her first meet. We then set a new goal of breaking 23:00. When she did that, we went to 22:30, which she also did. It motivates the runner to make new gains, while also building confidence.

Taking Bites Of The Elephant

There is an old saying, "taking a bite of the elephant." The elephant represents your large goal that you want to obtain. Since your goal is something big, the elephant is the animal chosen to symbolize that particular goal. Getting closer to your goal is taking a bite.

The bites symbolize progress. Any type of progress, no big or small, is still progress. Even running faster by one second is still a new personal best. I like to recognize all bites in meets, but I also like to do so in practice.

In interval training, when we run at goal pace, if an athlete was struggling to run a three-minute 800-meter, but then ran a 2:55, I am going to recognize that. Then, the athlete is aware they are making progress. The same goes for meets.

Say an athlete wants to run a 20:00 three mile. They run at 22:30 for their first meet. Their second meet they ran 22:18. We then tell them to try and break 22:00. Then, they go out and run at 21:58. We are breaking the whole elephant to smaller chunks, so that the goal does not appear to be overwhelming.

In my time, a lot of athletes will want to give up because they feel that what they want to accomplish is too far away. I like to use the driving analogy. Driving to Charleston from Peoria is a far drive, but I know I am closer once I get to Bloomington and Champaign. You have to chunk the goal and acknowledge the progress that is being made.

Motivating With Rewards

You are the boss, but you can still have fun. Athletes want to know they are doing a good job. I mean, they are the ones that are performing. For a smaller school, we do not have a lot of resources, so you have to be creative. These are some rewards that I use for the success of my team during the course of the season:

1. Verbal praise: I like to do this after the meet if an athlete runs a personal best. After the meet, we gather together for a closing. The parents are around, so they can hear the good news too.

2. Pie in the Face: We have a Run-A-Thon fundraiser where athletes ask for donations. We run around the track for 30 minutes and for each lap the runner runs, they receive a fixed amount (E.G $1 for 1 lap, $13 donation for 13 laps). We offer the kids a half day practice for $75 raised and for them to pie us in the face for $100 raised. For a team of 16 total runners, we raised $1,200 doing our run-a-thon. However, pieing us in the face was more fun for them.

3. Coach's Award: This is an award that I give at the end of the season directly from me. It's an award given to an athlete that demonstrates enthusiasm and never misses practice.

4. Most Improved Award: This is an award that we give for the most improved performance from one season to the next, or the beginning of the season to the end. I have done it either way. For example, we had an athlete who ran a 31:00 three mile his freshman year, and ran a 23:00 three mile his sophomore year. This is personally one of my favorite awards to give.

5. Most Valuable Runner: This is the MVP essentially. This is the award given to our best and most consistent runner. This does not necessarily mean your fastest runner. This is the runner who consistently places in the top tier of meets, and is essential to your team placing where it places.

Motivating For Life

I tell my athletes on a consistent basis that if they do not develop as an elite runner, I hope that they develop into an elite person. I love the success that comes with coaching my team, and I love watching my runners grow over the season. However, running will not be there entire life after they get out of high school.

Sure, some of them will run in college, but being responsible, respectful, and life-ready young men and women are more important. Our athletes will not learn all life skills through the sports, but there are some skills they can learn through your program.

Young people need to learn self-discipline and responsible behavior. Over the course of the season, they will face some form of adversity. Teaching them how to battle that adversity is a huge life skill that will go past high school.

The key is mutual respect. If you want your athletes to learn and grow, you must respect them, and they must respect you. The only way this will happen is by applying loving discipline. Kids will thrive in this coaching situation, and you will love watching them grow.

Chapter 3: Planning for Your High School Cross Country Season

You can have a great plan put together, but it will not matter if you do not have the personnel to carry it out. You need at least five members on a team to score, but you can have seven runs at a varsity meet. You will need to tap into all possible recruits no matter how large your school is. The more athletes you have, the bigger your family grows.

You also need to plan what kind of culture you want to have on your team. What expectations do you have? What are your expectations of a runner that joins? You will need to communicate that to the athletes that you recruit.

This chapter deals with recruiting and how you can get runners to join your program. This chapter will also give you some tips on expectation building. Also, we will begin discussing training plans for the summer and during the regular season.

Recruiting From The Bottom

There are many coaches that have an issue with getting talent out for their teams. Even I have issues with getting the top talent. My first year, I had to recruit athletes during the summer when we were not even in school. Luckily, I was the track coach the previous season, so I was in contact with a fair amount of track team. There are not always situations where you can luck out.

My first year I was able to recruit seven girls and five guys. Five of those girls were sprinters from our track team, and we used cross country as a strengthening for track season. That was one of my selling points for joining. You need to give kids a reason for wanting to join. Conditioning for basketball, for track, or just being healthy are some selling points I used my first year. I was able to expand on those as the years went on.

I have no qualifying standards to join my team. Some schools make cuts, but I feel the more runners the merrier. If I was at a larger school district, I would still not make any cuts because if someone wants to put the work in to run long distance, I will coach that person.

All in all, you need to figure out why someone should join your program. These are some recruiting points you can use for athletes you try and recruit:

Preparing For Basketball Season

Basketball season is right after the cross country season. In one of the towns I coach in, the basketball program is prevalent. The school recently won their 1,500th game in school history. Basketball is the sport that most boys want to play.

I use this more of a selling point for the boys. Girls can play volleyball in our area, and many of our girls who run track do not play basketball. However, there might be some for you in your area.

Cross country builds endurance and will help an athlete waltz into conditioning easily. Basketball requires a lot of running. I personally believe it helps with defense and your ability to play better on-the-ball defense. Most importantly, the athlete is doing something in the fall to stay in shape and get stronger.

I try to sell cross country as a sport that will help a boy's athleticism for basketball. Out of nine boys this past season, seven played basketball. If you look at their overall fitness from their freshman to sophomore years, every single one will tell you that they are faster and stronger from year one to year two. That reason is cross country.

Preparing For Track Season

For the sprinters, cross country is grueling. If you spent all of spring running nothing more than a 400 meter dash, running three miles is a huge step up. For the girls team, we usually have three to four sprinters come out that ran in our relays. This past track season, our 4X200 meter relay finished 11th in the state. One of those girls was a senior, but the other three came out for cross country because they want to run All-State this year.

Our true distance runners need cross country for track season, just like they need track for cross country season. Our state qualifier in the mile would have never made state if she did not put the work in running during the fall.

Building A Healthy Lifestyle

Each year, I have one to two runners that come out just to get a little healthy. They are some of my favorite runners. These runners are part of our "fun group." They do not have a lot of pressure because these runners know they are not there to compete competitively. However, you still set expectations and build goals because you want to see them reach their own success.

I usually look around for someone that is not active in a sport or a club, who would benefit from our atmosphere. The worst thing someone can do is just tell me they are not coming out. Last season, the kids recruited an athlete that was on the overweight side, and wanted to make a lifestyle change.

He ran all year and ran his for three mile race that season and he was so proud of himself. He later got hurt in the middle of the season and could not compete in many races, but he came to each practice. He cheered, walked, and biked with the kids. Overall, he was exercising.

I will never forget his senior night. He decided that even though he had not competed in three weeks, he was going to run. Our principal was our official. The last 400 meters, the principal and I ran with him. It was a rewarding experience for everyone.

Creating A Family

We talked a lot about goal setting in the previous chapters, so I want to talk about how we create a family. The runners that we recruit know each other for the most part, but they do not know each person. Think about it. You have runners that range from freshman to seniors. Plus, if you are in a co-op like us, you have athletes from two different schools.

I have some principles that I believe are important in creating a family atmosphere. There are five principles that come to mind and are laid out for you down below.

<u>Get To Know Your Teammates</u>

The first week I make the athletes get to know each other. I draw names from a hat and have groups run with each other. The number one runner could run with the slowest runner. That first week I do not care what the pace the kids are running. I want them to get to know their teammates. We preach that we are a family. You cannot feel like you are a part of a family if you do not know your family.

Supporting Your Teammates

The first practice we run our 202 Chaser. The team runs two 200-meter dashes to practice finishing a race on a grass surface. At the end, two athletes are chosen to run one more. One will go out and jog while the other will have to sprint and chase. When the "chaser" catches the other, the other runner sprints and the two race to the finish. The rest of the runners spread out all over the grass to cheer for the two runners.

I think this drill is important because it teaches finishing in a race, but every single member of the team is cheering for the runners. It makes each athlete feel like they are connected. Each runner will complete a chaser drill by week two. That way, each runner feels like their teammate has their back.

Be Cautious Of Negativity

Positive praise can travel fast, but a negative attitude can be super contagious. I had an athlete my first year that was negative everywhere she went. I pulled her aside one day and asked why she was even out if she did not want to be there. I was very blunt and said I will do whatever I can to help her with her outlook, but I would rather her not be around if she was going to be negative.

Communication goes a far way. She made a huge effort at correcting her attitude and members of the team noticed. What was great about this athlete is that when she was in a positive mood, the overall morale of the team was positive. When you have a happy consensus on the team, it will spread to all athletes.

It is important to pay attention to all athletes. If there is something that you can do to fix the mood, it is your obligation to your team to do so.

Resolve Conflicts As Quickly As Possible

My wife will be the first one to tell you that our biggest hurdle in our marriage is miscommunication. There will be times that we may have an issue, but we do not communicate that right way. I believe it is called the "snowball effect." Eventually, those little snowflakes (problems) roll into a giant snowball (even bigger problem).

Relationships are not the only place where a huge fight can occur. You are in charge of managing multiple personalities and forming a culture that everyone buys into. As much as you want each member of the team to be friends with each other, that will not be the case, even with the small schools.

What is important for us is that I make very clear that I have my captains handle any conflicts. I do not like to get involved unless I absolutely have to. I believe that when a captain handles the conflict, it teaches leadership to the captain, but also brings the team closer together. In my years, I have never had any conflicts that I needed to get involved in and that is a testament to handling our issues quickly.

Leave The Garbage In The Can

A lot can happen before a 3:30 p.m. practice. There is leaving the house, school, friends, and especially now with cell phones, social media. In other words, showing up to cross country in the right mentality may not always be the case.

In order to keep the peace, attitudes should be right before practices or meets. Again, when you get to know your athletes, you can sometimes tell when someone feels a little down. I am also in daily contact with my captains. They are the kids who are around the athletes during the day, so they usually hear what rumors are being said, if any.

I tell my team that when they are at practice, this is what their focus should be on. You will only perfect practice in the right mentality. Leave the garbage of the day in the garbage can.

Training Plans

The cross country season does not start that first week in August. The sport is year round when you factor track season which stretches from January to May. The most important months of cross country are during the summer. That is where your team will get the majority of your high mileage and long runs.

The IHSA gives us 30 contact days during the summer. These days I am allowed to be present and give instruction. The way we maneuver around these days is that I plan for the days. There are days where the kids just meet and run. These days are usually just recovery days.

The plan down below is a sample of what I do during the summer. You can modify the plan to your liking. Before you look at the plan, there are some terms that you need to understand. All paces are based on a one mile time trial.

Recovery Pace

This pace is an easy pace. This comes after hard workouts, or as filler workouts. You cannot run at max effort every day. You will injure yourself, but you still need to get miles in. This pace is usually two minutes to two and a half minutes slower than your goal three mile pace. This pace is conversation level. The athlete should be able to talk to a fellow runner as they complete the workout. To calculate your runner's recovery pace, add 2:20 to their goal mile time trial.

Tempo Pace

The tempo pace is a medium pace that brings an athlete to feeling uncomfortable, but also not too hard. The tempo pace is only used in spurts. For example, an athlete will run a specified amount of time and then have a rest. We run tempo workouts in minutes or distance. When calculating tempo pace, add 1:05 to their goal mile time.

5K And 10K Pace

The 5K pace is the goal three mile pace. In order to run your goal time, you have to practice running that three mile time pace. We set goals for a three mile time based on the mile time. If a runner runs between 5:30 and 5:45 for their mile time trial, we will set a goal for breaking 18:00 for the season.

The 10K pace is the next hardest pace. To calculate 10K pace, we add 45 seconds to the goal mile time. We usually run this pace uphill for a certain amount of distance. You can use the chart down below as a reference for the paces.

Pacing Chart

Goal Mile	Interval Pace	5K Pace	10K Pace	Tempo Pace	Recover Pace

	(400 and 800)				
5:30	1:22 (400) 2:03 (600) 2:55-3:00 (800)	6:00 mile pace	6:15 mile pace	6:35 mile pace	7:50 mile pace
5:45	1:25 (400) 2:07 (600) 3:00 to 3:07 (800)	6:15 mile pace	6:30 mile pace	6:50 mile pace	8:07 mile pace

6:00	1:30 (400)	6:30 mile pace	6:45 mile pace	7:05 mile pace	8:27 mile pace
	2:15 (600)				
	3:07 to 3:13) (800)				

Summer Plan

Now that you have had a chance to review some of the terms associated with the plans, down below you will see how summer plans work. The plan has the athletes run six times a week. On the days that feature less mileage, I plan for the athletes to run those workouts when I am not around. There are days that "core" and "roller recovery" will be mentioned, and I would like to take a moment to explain those terms as well.

When it says core, we take 10-15 minutes to perform a variety of strengthening exercises for the legs or core muscles. We do this to prevent injuries. There are many muscles being used. By practicing supplemental core exercises, we have never had an injury in all my years coaching. I try to switch up the core exercises, but some examples can include planks, pushups, single leg squats, vertical jumps, etc.

We possess three foam rollers, and one large form roller. Plus, we have two tennis balls. On those days, I make sure the athletes use the foam roller for recovery. These devices help tighten the muscles and then release blood flow. Again, you have to take care of your body. The athlete will unlikely do it on their own, so I make sure they take the time.

First Week	4 miles recovery pace, Core
	2 mile warmup 3X800s uphill at 10K Pace, 3X800 down rest 2 mile cooldown Bands
	6 mile recovery pace, Core
	4 mile recovery pace, Roller Recovery
	2 mile warmup 3 mile tempo pace

	2 mile cooldown Roller Recovery
	9 miles recovery pace
Second Week	5 miles recovery pace, Core
	2 mile warmup 6-5-4-3-2-1 min tempo pace with 1 min rest 2 mile cooldown Bands
	7 miles recovery pace, Core
	5 miles recovery pace, Roller Recovery
	2 mile warmup 1-2-3-4-4-3-2-1 at 10K Pace with 1 min rest 2 mile cooldown Roller Recovery
	10 miles recovery pace
Third Week	6 miles recovery pace,

	core
	2 mile warmup 4X800s uphill at 10K pace, 4X800s down rest 2 mile cooldown Bands
	8 miles recovery pace, Core
	6 miles recovery pace, Roller Recovery
	2 mile warmup 4 mile tempo pace 2 mile cooldown Roller Recovery
	11 miles recovery pace
Fourth Week	3 miles recovery pace, core, Roller
	1 mile warmup 6-5-4-3-2-1 min at 5K

	pace with 1 min rest 1 mile cooldown
	6 miles recovery pace
	3 miles recovery pace, core, Roller Recovery
	1 mile warmup 3 miles Tempo Pace 1 mile cooldown
	Rest
Fifth Week	3 miles recovery pace, core, Roller *RECOVERY WEEK*
	1 mile warmup 6-5-4-3-2-1 min at 5K pace with 1 min rest 1 mile cooldown
	6 miles recovery pace
	3 miles recovery pace, core, Roller Recovery
	1 mile warmup

	3 miles Tempo Pace 1 mile cooldown
	Rest
Sixth Week	6 miles recovery pace, core
	2 mile warmup 5X800s uphill at 10K pace with 800 down rest 2 mile cooldown Bands
	8 miles recovery pace, core
	6 miles recovery pace, core
	2 mile warmup, 4 mile tempo pace (1 mile tempo, ½ mile rest), 2 mile cooldown, Roller Recovery
	12 miles recovery pace
Seventh Week	8 miles recovery pace, core

	2 mile warmup, 4 mile fartlek (3 min 10K pace, 2 min recovery pace) 2 mile cooldown, Bands
	9 miles recovery pace, core
	8 miles recovery pace, roller recovery
	3 mile warmup 6-5-4-3-2-1 at 5K pace with 1 min rest 2 mile cooldown, Roller Recovery
	13 mile recovery pace
Eighth Week	9 miles recovery pace
	9 miles recovery pace
	10 miles recovery pace
	3 mile warmup 1-2-3-4-4-3-2-1 at 5k pace with 1 min rest 3 mile cooldown

	8 miles recovery pace
	15 miles recovery pace
Ninth Week **No Contact Period**	3 miles recovery pace, core, Roller *RECOVERY WEEK*
	1 mile warmup 6-5-4-3-2-1 min at 5K pace with 1 min rest 1 mile cooldown
	6 miles recovery pace
	3 miles recovery pace, core, Roller Recovery
	1 mile warmup 3 miles Tempo Pace 1 mile cooldown
	Rest
	4 miles recovery pace Racing drills core

Long Range Plan (In Season)

Once you have completed your summer training, the season will begin. You will have to modify the plan to fit your athlete's best needs. For athletes that did not train, I shortened the running for them. You need to use your best judgement.

A typical day starts with announcements. That is followed with warmup drills, and stretching. We then do 6X100 meter drills that focus on racing tactics. These can include cutting in, turning around sharp corners, or running former. We then do the main workout provided in the table. The day will end with some core, or 3X300 meter chaser drills. We end with a team stretch and a team break. The break is usually our motto, which is Wild Rockets.

Day	Workout
First Week	1 mile time trial
*We start the season officially on a Wednesday the second week of August	10X400s at goal three mile pace with 1 min rest
	10 Miles at recovery pace
	30 min-30 min-15 min
	10-10-5-5-5-4-4-2 at fartlek pace with 1 min rest

Second Week	30X200s with 1 min rest
	1-1-2-2-3-3-4-4-5-5-8-8-4-4-2 with 1 min rest WL
	10X800s with 2 min rest
	30 minute run-uniforms WL
	1 mile time trial, 10 min recovery, 10X400s, 10X200s
	14 miles
Third Week	30 min sprint 50, jog 60
	45 min-30 min-15 min with 5 min rest
	30X200s, 1 min rest
	45-30-30
	7X1200s with 4 min rest
	15 miles
Fourth Week	1-1-2-2-3-3-4-4-6-6-4-4-2-2-2-2-1-1 with 1 min rest
	45-45-30 (IVC Meet)-We use this meet as practice, just to get miles

	in
	25X400s with 1 min rest
	10-10-5-5-5-4-4-2 with 1 min rest w 300s
	1 hour fartlek
	Charleston Invite
Fifth Week	Labor Day No Practice
	5X1 mile repeat with 3 min rest
	4 sets of 5X200s with 1 min rest, then 30-15
	Scavenger Hunt core
	1-1-2-2-2-2-4-6-6-4-2-2-2-2-1-1 roller recovery
	Princeton Invite
Sixth Week	20X400s with 1 min rest
	10X800s with 2 min rest
	Peoria Meet

	4X long hills
	6X200s
	Bureau Valley Invite
Seventh Week	3X1 mile with 3 min rest
	Princeville Meet + 30
	45-30-30
	4 set of 5X200s, 1 min rest, 30-30-15
	45 min run
	Kewanee Invite
Eighth Week	6X200s
	Tri County Conference Meet
	6X800s at goal mile pace
	4 set of 5X200s with 1 min rest, 30-15
	Rest

	Elmwood Invite
Ninth Week	45-30-30
	LWRB Invite
	3X400s very fast with 3 min between
	2 mile time trial on track, 15 min recovery, 2 one mile repeat
	4X400s on Regional like course
	Prairie Central Invite-As you please
Tenth Week	Amboy Invite
	4 set of 5X200, then 30-15
	45-30-15
	3X400s very fast
	6X200s
	Peoria Heights Invite
Postseason	1 mile time trial, 1 mile fast

Week (11th Week)	2 set of 5X200s, 15 min
	45-30-15
	3X400s very fast
	Rest
	Regional

If I have any athletes make the Sectional, which we have, I usually just repeat the 11th week, but I will change the mile time trial to a different speed workout that prepares them for the course. Assuming we have any athletes make the state tournament, we will not run any speed that week, and the athlete will have two days of rest.

I am going to provide another plan. As I said in the earlier chapters, my first year, we were not as talented in terms of our distance runners. I used this plan for them, which I would recommend for beginners. This plan helped the athletes become better distance runners even though they were not your typical distance runner.

8-9	Wednesday	Easy 3-4, Cardio Power
8-10	Thursday	Easy 3-4, Plyo Circuit

8-11	Friday	Medium 4-5, Bands, Iron Core
8-12	Saturday	90 Minute Run
8-14	Monday	Easy 50-60 minutes, Plyo Circuit
8-15	Tuesday	4X Mile Repeats, Bands, Iron Core
8-16	Wednesday	Easy 60 minutes, Cardio Circuit
8-17	Thursday	Oregon Drills- 40 minutes, Bands, Iron Core
8-18	Friday	Easy 40 minutes,
8-19	Saturday	90 Minute run
8-21	Monday	Easy 50-60 minutes,
8-22	Tuesday	1000 meter on, 200 meter off, 6-8 sets, bands, iron core

8-23	Wednesday	Easy 60 minutes, cardio circuit
8-24	Thursday	Ultimate frisbee/soccer
8-25	Friday	Easy 40 minute, interval circuit
8-26	Saturday	90 minute long run, grill out party
8-28	Monday	50-60 minute easy, plyo circuit
8-29	Tuesday	IVC Meet
8-30	Wednesday	Easy 4-5 mile fartlek, 3 minute easy, 1 hard,
8-31	Thursday	Oregon drills 40 minutes, bands, iron core
9-1	Friday	Easy 40 minutes, bands
9-2	Saturday	Meet at Charleston

9-5	Tuesday	50-60 minute easy, 3 minutes on, 3 minutes off, plyo circuit
9-6	Wednesday	4X Mile repeat, bands, iron core
9-7	Thursday	4 miles, 800 on, 800 off, cardio circuit-track
9-8	Friday	Easy 40 minutes, bands, iron core
9-9	Saturday	Meet at Princeton
9-11	Monday	50-60 minute, 5 minutes on, 2 minutes off, plyo circuit
9-12	Tuesday	1000 meter on, 200 meter job, 6-8 sets, bands, iron core
9-13	Wednesday	Easy 4-5 mile fartlek, 3 minute easy, 1:30 hard,

		bands
9-14	Thursday	Princeville Meet
9-15	Friday	OFF
9-16	Saturday	Meet at Bureau Valley
9-18	Monday	50-60 minute easy. 3 minutes on, 3 minute off, plyo circuit
9-19	Tuesday	4X mile repeats, bands, iron core
9-20	Wednesday	40 minute easy, cardio circuit
9-21	Thursday	Meet at Putnam County
9-22	Friday	40 minute easy, bands, iron core
9-23	Saturday	60 minute long run on own
9-25	Monday	Oregon drills
9-26	Tuesday	Meet at Tri County

		Conference
9-27	Wednesday	Cardio circuit, ultimate frisbee
9-28	Thursday	45 minutes, 5 minutes on, 2 off
9-29	Friday	1000 meter on, 200 jog, 5X, bands, iron core
9-30	Saturday	60 minute long run
10-2	Monday	50-60 minute run easy, 3 minute on, 2 minute off plyo circuit
10-3	Tuesday	Meet at Roanoke
10-4	Wednesday	40 minute fartlek, minute easy, 1:30 hard, cardio circuit
10-5	Thursday	Oregon drills, bands, iron core
10-6	Friday	OFF

10-7	Saturday	Meet at Prairie Central
10-9	Monday	40 minute run, 3 minute on, 1 minute off bands, iron core
10-10	Tuesday	Meet at Heyworth Invite
10-11	Wednesday	40 minute run, cardio circuit
10-12	Thursday	Scavenger Hunt, bands
10-13	Friday	OFF
10-14	Saturday	Meet at Peoria Heights
10-16	Monday	40 minute easy run, bands, core
10-17	Tuesday	1600 time trial, 3 sets of 1600 meter drill, core
10-18	Wednesday	Game
10-19	Thursday	40 minutes easy

10-20	Friday	Off and spaghetti supper/game night
10-21	Saturday	Meet at Regional

Bands Training

We incorporate band training within our workouts to avoid injuries. Bands are cheap and can be used for the upper and lower body. There are five main moves that we use during cross country season.

- Straight leg outs: The band is around the ankles. When laying on one side, raise the leg up to make a 45-degree angle in between your legs. Then place the leg back down. We do this 25 times for each side.

- Knee extension: The band is around the ankles. While laying on your back. Bring your feet closer to your butt, while your knees remain up. Extend one leg straight out, bringing tension to the band. Repeat 25 times for each leg.

- Straight leg raise ups: The band is around the ankles. You sit on your butt, while sitting straight up. Your legs are extended out. Lift your ankle straight up, while keeping the other leg on the ground. Repeat 25 times for each leg.

- Basketball defensive stance: The band is around the ankles. While standing up, slightly bend your knees and get in a defensive stance. Have one leg shift outward in the right or left direction, while keeping the other leg planted. Then, bring the other leg in to release the tension. Go one direction five times and then back to the starting point. Do this five sets total.

- Clams: The band is around the knees. Lay on your back and turn your torso, so that one knee is laying on the ground. Place the knee on top of that other knee. Use your hip to extend the knee up and down. Do this 25 times for each side.

Conclusion

In conclusion, there are two types of plans that a coach can use to coach their athletes. You will have to tailor your plan to the group that you are coaching. Make sure to include some type of strengthening and core exercises to avoid injuries.

Chapter 4: Teaching And Improving Performance In High School Cross Country

We have discussed the training plans in the last chapter, but running cross country is more than just running the miles. One underlooked aspect of running is proper running form. Athletes do not just use their legs to get from one point to another. It is your job as a coach to teach proper running mechanics, and improve the performance of your athletes.

A runner's basic form will have been imprinted before your athlete reaches high school. That does not mean that the form will be ideal. Teaching how to run up and down hills will be included in this chapter, as well as how to properly run a successful kick.

Teaching Form

More experienced coaches will have heard of the saying, "run tall." The saying derives from the famous University of Oregon coach, Bill Bowerman. When an athlete runs upright, they are forward. The runner does not lean forward, or backward, but will keep their body over their feet. This keeps the runner balanced when running through various terrain on cross country courses. When a runner is upright, overstriding does not become an issue.

A common flaw that runners make is not using proper arm action. Do not let the hands swing across your upright position. Arms should be kept down low near the hip level. The best runners will have their arms slightly bent at the elbows. When we want to move faster, we tell our athletes to "chicken wing and go."

In summary, these are some of the basics that a coach should teach when perfecting an ideal running form:

1. Head position: Look straight ahead and never at the ground. When a runner is looking down at the ground, the runner will run slower. Also, when the runner is looking down, the neck will feel fatigued, but will also make it much harder for the athlete to breathe in any oxygen.

2. Body angle: Keep the body balanced over the legs. While running uphill, the runner should lean with the whole body. Imagine a line is running through your body, and you must keep the vertical line. When running downhill, keep the body perpendicular to the ground. By running tall, you will not lose speed.

3. Arm position: Carry the arms at a lower position, and angled at the elbows. Use your elbows to move the arms back and forth. Stay away from swinging the arms back and forth. Never let the hands swing across the center of your chest. The shoulders should not move. You want all limbs to be moving forward.

4. Hands: Keep your hands relaxed. This means never clenching your hands to make a fist. When the hands are clenched, the upper body

creates tension, and this does not help the runner remain relaxed.

5. Footplant: Land on the lower ball of the foot. Never land on the toes and this will lead to shin splints. Do not let the heel smack the foot. We preach that we try to practice soft landing. We want a quiet landing, which helps practice soft impact.

6. Stride length: We do not want to over stride. Avoid reaching for the next stride. With a low, forward leg lift, over striding should not be a problem. The longer the distance, the shorter the stride.

7. Breathing: A runner should breathe deeply, regularly, and inhale and exhale through the nose and the mouth. When a runner only breathes through the mouth, the diaphragm is not opening all the way. Plus, you are more susceptible to cramps.

8. Relaxation: Avoid unnecessary tension and stress. Let the lower jaw feel relaxed. When I feel tense, a little wiggle of the jaw can do wonders. We tell athletes to take a deep breath and drop the shoulders in the middle of races to relax the upper body. Another sign of tension is in the hands. If the arms tire, drop and "shake it out."

Teaching Cross Country Form

First of all, we never practice running in spikes. When teaching how to run, we practice on areas that are set up for the course that we run on that week. If we are running on a flat course, we will run maybe intervals on the track. If we are running at a hilly course, we will run hill repeats leading up to the race.

Hill running is beneficial in terms of teaching athletes to run with perfect form. Joe Newton, the legendary York High School coach, told his athletes to "attack the hill." In simpler terms, the faster you get up the hill, the less time you are on the hill.

When attacking the hill, a runner should lean forward with their chest. Shorten your stride, and drive more with the knees. Try and pass anyone around to give some internal motivation. There will be some runners that are not mentally ready to take on hills. It is important to teach how to mentally attack the hill as well. Do not go into the hill with the mentality of, "when is this going to end?" Attack the hill with the mentality of "I am going to pass as many people as I can."

For downhill running, our runners usually have a better attitude. We tell our runners to fly down the hill. We want to get down the hill as quickly as possible. Slightly lean forward, keeping the body perpendicular to the ground. Do not let the runner lean back, as this leads to a hard pounding on the terrain. Runners can still go down fast when running forward, but we try to take on a smoother approach.

Teach Breathing and Pace Changing

In the earlier part of this chapter, we briefly talked about breathing mechanics. The runner should breathe through their nose and their mouth. This maximizes the amount of oxygen that goes into the lungs, and avoids cramps.

I usually have the athletes do this simulation at the beginning of the season. I have the runners place their hand on their stomach. I first have the runners breathe in only through their mouth. The stomach will slightly move in and out. Then, I have the runner breathe in through their nose and out with their mouth. The change in distance is astounding because by doing this, much more oxygen is circulating.

Runners do not need to count breaths or time their footsteps. There are two types of minds. If a runner does not like to focus on their breathing, I have the runner focus on their arm placement and the breathing will take care of itself. For others that need to refocus, I tell the runners to focus on their breathing. Every mind is different.

Pace changing is very important for the beginning of the race. Most of the time, runners get out too fast. We run a drill that teaches pace changing. We run the first 50 meters hard, but then have the runners change to their 5K interval pace. However, you hope that the athlete can turn on the fast pace at the end of the race.

We practice our kick with our 202s at the end. The athletes run two hard 200 meter sprints and use visualization techniques to pass potential runners. If you do not practice "kicking," then you cannot expect the athlete to have a stellar kick in a race.

Improving Runner Performance

Style points are never awarded to cross country runners; however, there are no points awarded for starting a race in first place. Runners who are young on experience, but huge on enthusiasm will start like a horse out of a gate and then slog their way into the finish line. The fact of the matter is that pacing out a race is a challenge and takes time to develop.

As a coach, you want your runners to spread their energy over the course of the entire distance. You almost want a clock in their head pacing themselves as they race. We want runners who can be strong for the entire race and to finish near the top to earn their top accolades.

Pacing is one of the single most hardest tactics to coach, but is one of the most rewarding things to see when your athlete masters it.

Improving Pacing With A Plan

We provide our athletes with a plan. We do not want our athletes to go out too fast at the beginning.

The race was not won in the beginning. The race can be lost there. We want our athletes to be in place for the hunt at the end rather than falling off midway. A fast early pace can kill off the runners who attempt it. Some athletes will need convincing that this is the tactic to follow, but if they do not follow this way, they will be in agony.

How do we improve our race pacing? For starters, runners need to understand that they do not want to run their first mile in six minutes, second mile in seven minutes, and third mile in eight minutes. "Negative splits" is a term you want your athletes to get used to hearing. This means that the second half of the race is faster than the first half of the race. We have our runners hold back at the start of the race, but not too much. Even if the runner goes down five second each mile, it still counts.

How do you practice negative splits? Conditions on a course are usually consistent, so we can break apart a target time by the interval of 200s. We normally do not have runners use a watch during meets, but this is when the watch can be an integral part of practice.

Say a runner wants to run a time of 17:00, which is a 5:40 mile pace. We develop a chart with the runners' names on it. We then break down a "target time" they want to hit every quarter of the mile. We look at the course map and determine where these markers are. If an athlete does their homework, they will know roughly where each part of the race is. At practice, we can pick an area to run and mark it down when we do our interval training.

Coaches and managers can stand at certain marks and keep times silently or aloud, pending how you want to coach. If we do it silently and show the athletes after, it may change their mentality of how they think. They can reflect and wonder if they were going too fast or too slow. Older runners tend to understand more about pacing as the year goes on.

Example Pace Chart

	1/4	1/2	¾	1	1 1/4	1 1/2	1 3/4	2	2 1/4	2 1/2	2 3/4	3
Smith	85 sec	2:48	4:12	5:37	7:01	8:30	10:06	11:31	13:01	14:25	15:39	17:00

Finishing The Kick

As discussed earlier in this chapter, high schoolers will start off too fast. We want to finish fast from the second half to the end. Races are won in the middle. We want the middle mile to be our fastest mile if possible. That is the mile that we want to run the hardest. By passing runners in the middle of the race, you don't just give yourself confidence, but you hurt the mental psyche of the runners that you pass.

We want to set ourselves up for the opportunity to be in a position to win. The last 200 meters of a 400-meter dash are a dog fight, just like the last 400 meters of the mile. It's not any different in cross country. A well-prepared runner will start to accelerate with a quarter of a mile to go. The big kick should begin about 300 meters left. The late Joe Newton once said, "Nobody passes you in the last 150. Run with reckless abandon." That is how your runners should be as well.

Chapter 5: Teaching Race Strategy In High School Cross Country

If you really think about it, cross country is essentially two events into one. There's the individual race. The race that you the individual has to run and conquer. There's also the team aspect, as your individual finish impacts the points towards the team place. In the previous chapter, we talked about how to improve your individual performance. Now, we talk about running together to minimize team points. Cross country is a rare sport, where less is more.

Cross country is an unusual sport to coach. Other teams have 10 to 22 players on the field at one time. In this field, you compete with 25 other teams with 200 runners on the field. In the biggest stage, only your top seven will run for you. Because of this crowd, team tactics come into play more than they do in other sports. Runners and coaches from championship teams tell you that the team's finish means more than the individual, but how do you get that philosophy across with a full buy-in?

Developing Individual Tactics

You might be thinking to yourself, didn't I just read that the team finish is what we want? Yes, you are absolutely correct; however, we can't get the team to finish without the individual. After all, the individual is running the race, so they need to understand how to run strategically. You may be the coach, but you are not always going to be around at every turn. The runner needs to understand how to run without you around to coach them. Once the individual conquers the run, your team finish will come too.

Individual Racing Tips

- Avoid starting too fast. Make a move throughout the race.

- If you know the trail is narrow (meaning passing is hard), start off fast, and then settle.

- When you become out of sight, speed your pace quickly. Discourage the runner and make him think he's lost ground.

- On windy days, run closely behind the runner in front of you. Let them absorb the wind.

- If you run behind an athlete, never look at their feet. Keep your head up and be engaged in what is happening.

- Pay attention to high arms. If your opponent raises their arms, assume they are getting tired. Make a move.

- When passing an opponent, give off the impression you are fresh. Make them think you are the stronger one.

- "Flush Out," which means increasing the pace for a few strides. Use this to gain a physical and mental lift midway through the race.

- At the finish, you are a sprinter. Pretend that the finish line is 10 yards past where the actual finish line is.

Pack Running

Team is by far the more important aspect of cross country. We have made that perfectly clear by now. The team that trains together races together. In order to get every individual to run well on your team, the idea of pack running should be used.

Our athletes warm up together, run intervals together, and cool down together. The top seven run as a group, while the others stay within their own groupings. Heck, your number eight, nine, or ten runners may push themselves more in order to run with the top group. Our runners will always encourage each other. There is a sense of family involved.

At meets, ideally the runners stay bunched together. It doesn't always work that way. You don't want your faster runners falling back to run with your "slower" runners. However, you build that idea into your No. 5, No. 6, and No. 7 runner that you want them up near the pack, which could help the overall team finish.

We don't expect everyone to come across the finish line at the same time, but we put emphasis on the time spread between all scorers. Some advice would be a 30 second difference. If that's the case, your team looks pretty good.

Setting Team Goals

The individual should have a personal goal, but if you can get the member to buy into the team's success, everything will fall into place. You want the runner to agree that the team is more important. After all, cross country is half mental.

What's great about our runners is that when they cross the finish line, they take a breath and immediately run to the finish area to cheer on their teammates. When the race is over, they are asking questions like "How did the team do?", "Did we win?", "Did _____ PR?" That makes me as a coach incredibly happy.

This may not be a "racing tactic," but by setting this mindset, you are making the individual a better teammate. In my opinion, if they are a great teammate, they will be a great runner, and improve their performance on game day. It's a distraction, but the best kind.

Developing Race Tactics

When we go to a meet, we have to be smarter runners. We could have the most athletic kids on the field, but if they do not run with a plan, they will burn out and fizzle to the ground. There are three phases to a race: start, middle, and end. Since there are just three miles in a race, you get the idea.

Start Tactics

As mentioned before, we want to avoid starting off too fast. Most athletes go out like a bat out of hell. They run the first 100 meters in an all-out sprint, or they get caught up with the adrenaline rush. Think about it, if your best boy runs the first ¼ of the race at 60 seconds, he is on pace for a 4-minute mile pace. That's Olympic level racing there, and these kids are aged between 15-18.

We obviously can't simulate mass starts at practice, but we can work on steady pacing. We never want to be in front at the beginning. Count one-thousand-one up to ten at the beginning of the race. Here are two major advantages for doing this:

1. It eliminates a sprint start, jog for recovery, and middle burnout. This way, we can steady pace ourselves throughout the race because we didn't burn out all of our energy at the beginning of the race.

2. It allows our runners to be near our teammates. Without the delayed start, we lose our "pack." Our teammates have trained together all year, and running side by side gives them a sense of security.

Middle Tactics

Runners do not pass us during the middle. That's our job. It's more fun to pass someone in the middle of the race than the beginning. You gain a mental edge over your opponent too. It also builds a sense of momentum. If you are going to pass someone, you do it with authority. Let them know this is "your trail."

From a team aspect, you are only as good as your fifth runner. The top three runners will take care of business most of the time. If we are at an invite, I will spend some extra time with our fourth and fifth runner, making sure we are getting every point we can get. When you pack five runners near the top, you are hard to beat.

Kicking At The End

The final mile is a dogfight. We want to continue to make moves and pass with authority. At this point, your body is tired. We practice "shaking out" our body during the second half of the race. Every couple of minutes, we want our athletes to take a deep breath, drop the shoulders, and relax the upper body. This could be every turn, straight, or whatever interval you want for your runners. In the end, we want to have enough to kick.

The final ½ mile should be viewed as an accelerating kick. The second to last 400 meters, you are accelerating your pace just a bit. The runner should have their shoulders down, arms at a chicken wing, and a strong knee drive. The final 400 meters, the runner is building nearly 80% of what they have left. The 300 meter mark should be 90%, and the last 200 meters is an all out sprint. We practice this with 2X300s at the end of practice to simulate our finish.

Developing Race Plans

I tend to scout the opponents at our meet prior to the meet. I have learned that some runners do better when they are assigned a runner to beat. When you run enough meets, you get to be on a first name basis with other kids from other teams. It's nothing personal, it's just competition and most of the time the kids understand that. We tend to do this at smaller meets though. At larger meets, this tactic is impossible.

In larger meets, we tell the runners to "run your own race and stick to the plan." Knowing the competition is important, but it's not always going to work. At bigger races, you can't find that rival that you have been racing all season. They are going to get lost in the crowd. We already have an idea of how we match up with them. Run your race, and that person might show up.

Before races, I will also post times for that given course and compare it to other courses to give the runners an idea. I want them to know who ran what, so they can build a sense of confidence. I don't do this to psyche them out. I want the runners to know they can run a time I want them to run, or place higher than what they expected.

Conclusion

The runner has to have a plan. This isn't basketball, where we can run an isolation play to our best player. We could have the state's best runner. If he isn't prepared for the competition, course, and himself, we are doomed from the start.

Chapter 6: Mentally Preparing For Meets In High School Cross Country

Training is vital to a successful season, but this chapter is not going to be about training. We talked about racing tactics in the previous chapter, and those are crucial, but I want to talk about something that is equally important.

You have likely picked up by now that cross country is half mental. You have likely read subliminal messages about how a certain approach can affect the mental side. This chapter is going to be all about the mental and logistical preparation for a competition.

The tactics offered are for the biggest race of the season. For you that could be state, conference, or an invitation that is close to your heart. Regardless, when it comes to the biggest meet of the year, the training tapers down. Your role at this time is to bring the runners to their physical and mental peak. In the final days, or hours, before "the big one," you make that final climb towards the top of the mountain.

Building Up Your Psyche

You want to work on the runner's minds for a whole week leading up to the race. At this time, guest speakers are a great way to get the team ready. I went to high school with an all-state runner that would come in and speak to our runners about what worked for him. This is always a great approach, especially since they went through the grind. An outside voice can get to a runner sometimes.

If you are preparing for the postseason, your runners that aren't in the top seven might be done. Not for us. It's tradition that the season ends for everyone, when the season ends for everyone. Our runners who aren't as fast have a critical role. They are used to build up our athletes at the top and they know that. Having support like that pushes someone to their best level and we want to be the best before the biggest race of the year.

Other Tips

- Dress for success: We have the kids dress up for school. I even wear a tie.

- Report to school 30 minutes extra early.

- Designate a hype guy/girl: This means someone that is "over the top" on excitement.

- Bring a speaker: At your camp, play appropriate hype music.

- Make a connection: A personal story from you can set the mood. Once I told my team I knew how scared they were of failure because I was scared of fatherhood. It's amazing how a little bit of vulnerability can bring up someone else.

Chapter 7: Evaluating Yourself As A Coach In High School Cross Country

Once the race begins, you are a spectator. You are a highly interested fan. You can't call timeouts to discuss race strategy. You have to trust that everything you have preached will be followed on game day.

Once the gun fires, you runners are on their own. You will only see them at select points, which can be maybe 2-3 times in a race. When you talk to them at the finish line, it will be too late to change anything that happened during the race, so how do we properly coach at a cross country meet?

Coaching At The Meet

When you are at the meet, you do not just have one duty. There are several. In this section, we will outline your tasks of coaching the course, your overall duty, making comments, and coaching after the meet.

Coaching On The Course

As your runners head to the starting line, you can expect emotions to range from nervous to excited. They have a race plan that they developed with you, but you must also have a plan. What's great about coaching cross country, is that you will be moving all over the place.

To start, I try to spend as much time with the runners before the gun goes off. When the runners are warming up, I will stand around the area. We talk about anything that is not related to the race. They know our plan, and talking about everything 10 minutes beforehand is not going to do much good. I would rather them be focused and relaxed.

Since I am much more mobile, I find the halfway marks for each mile and try to group with them. I have my assistant coach and managers get mile splits. I can't coach and give comments with a big crowd. They are not going to hear me, so I try and find spots that are less crowded.

I especially want to find a spot where I think they should begin their kick. I cheer as loud as I can to get them started. I hope they can hold that up towards the end when they see the larger crowd. Once they see all the people at the end, their adrenaline will kick in and everything happens after just happens.

Coaching Duties

You have to accept there is not a whole lot you can do during the race. For the fastest boys, this race could last just 17 minutes. There are some duties that you can serve to your kids during this small time sample.

For starters, I try to let the runners know if they are on pace or not during the first half mile. This allows them to understand if they got out too fast. Remember, we want our runners to control the middle and kick at the end.

During the race, I like to give the kids checkpoints just as reminders. The race is a mental sport. If my runners know that the second mile is coming up, or they are halfway done with the first mile, it brings a sense of relief. Sometimes, we get lost in our mind when we are running. We need a mental stimulus to keep us in the game.

Another duty you should expect is to take the times of your runners. You do not want to go to a meeting with no time recorded. It happens out of human nature, but if you can prevent it, then do it. I've been fortunate that I have an assistant coach take care of that hurdle. If you don't have an assistant coach, bring a few extra kids who didn't run that day. Kids are always eager to help if you give them a role and make them feel valued.

Finally, keep a record of personal bests. At the end, if one of your runners runs a best time, give them the recognition they deserve. It feels good to announce the times to the runners at the end and see their faces light up when they run their best.

Coaching Comments

Be positive and honest. It's really that simple. At practice, I am hard on my athletes, but they respect me. Even on the days where they are the most mad at me, I know that later in the afternoon, we can share a laugh. We can do this because deep down they know I want what is best for them, and I will always be honest with them.

Nobody can handle negativity all the time. In a race, they are already giving their bodies up for a challenge. Throwing negativity into their mind is not going to do anything to help them get over a hurdle. You need to build the runners up. Say things like, "This is going to be your day," "I believe in you, and I need you to believe in yourself," or "You are going to rock this!"

While we should never demean our runners, it's important to note that you should never demean other teams. Jealousy of great teams is naturally human; however, we are in this together. What makes me proud of our kids is that we cheer on all runners, especially the schools we see a lot during the season. That's how we build more connections and relationships.

I have a very strict policy about bullying. If I catch any wind, you are gone. They go the same for adults. You as the coach lead by example. Cheer on other teams if you recognize kids at larger meets. If your kids need support during this season, expect other teams to do too. After all, this is supposed to be fun.

Coaching Afterwards

Since girls run first, they get the shorter end of the stick. When the girls are done running, they are expected to get a short cooldown, and then cheer on the boys. The boys have it easier, and cheer for the girls first and do not have to rush their cooldown. This is just one of our routines after a race is completed.

When the boys are done, I have the girls jog out with the boys. We are a family, so I think it is important to have the family go out and calm down their bodies. It's important to never skip the cooldown, but it's more enjoyable with more people.

After the cooldown, I will talk to the runners for a few minutes. I highlight the positives and the need to work ons. I always end with PRs because you should always end on a positive note. We should never end on the negatives because they will think they did not perform well. Always end with a positive because they will help build their mental performance moving forward, which will translate to physical success as well.

Your job does not end there. I will sometimes talk to parents and tell the parents of the kids who had a good meet to be proud. Remember, the kids go home with the parents when the meet is over. If they are telling the runner positive parts of the meet, they are aiding you in building up their confidence. You don't have to tell a parent that their kid did a good job at every meet. Pick your spots because it will mean more when you do.

Coaching Evaluation

One of my former runners spoke at graduation, and it was one of the greatest moments of my coaching life. I would like to share what she said in part of her speech:

"High school has been a challenge in my life, but it has taught me a few things. I know that life is not something handed to you. I know that you have to earn what you want. I know that feeling is amazing, like getting a "Daubs Hug" after proving you could do something. I want to live that way after high school. I want to always earn my dreams."

Right after graduation, she gave me a full copy of the speech she wrote. I still have it to this day as one of my favorite keepsakes. Coaching cross country is fun, but I tell my runners that I want them to be better people than athletes. That is something I take very seriously in my reflection as a coach. Did I teach the skills and make these kids better, but did I also help them become a better person?

Evaluating Runners' Performance

One beauty about cross country is that you have a simple statistic to measure the growth of your athletes: time. Being able to measure the performance of a runner from their August time to their October time is something special.

We have other standards too. How fast did they run this year versus last? How much did they improve during the season? A runner that improves in any capacity wins. The greater the progress, the greater the win. Even if the growth is not as big as their peers, it's still winning in my book. If the athlete went out and gave the sport their best try, then you should be proud of them and make them aware of that.

Evaluating Awards

We have several awards that we give out at the end of the season. There are the Coach's Award, Most Improved Award, and Most Valuable Runner Award.

The Coach's Award is an award directly given by my assistant coach and myself. Some of the characteristics we look at include their work ethic, personality during the season, and attitude. We really look at how someone acted during the season. In the past, I have given this award to fast and slow athletes. Their common theme was that they supported every teammate and tried to be their true family member.

The Most Improved Award goes to someone that exceeded your expectations. The name is pretty self explanatory, but I will give an example anyways. I had a runner go out his freshman year. He was a little overweight and ran his first race in over 30 minutes.

He almost quit after the first race, but he stuck with it. He came back out his sophomore season, and ran a three-mile of 22-minutes. For someone who ran the spot to get healthy, stuck with it, and was a great teammate, he deserved this award.

The Most Valuable does not meet that this runner is the fastest at every meet. This runner is someone that is the most dependable and gets the job done at every meet. They are our "rock." They are someone you can always count on. We have given this award to our second-fastest runner before because we knew they would be near the top-10 every time, even though he clocked in the second-fastest time all season.

We also give letter awards and pins based on the letter policy of the school. If you have a JV team, I would insist on giving your JV awards as well.

For my seniors, I tend to say something extra special at our awards night. I want the parents to know what it's been like coaching them the last four years. You sort of grow up with the kids and it hurts when they leave. For the runners that want to run in college, I do everything I can to find a coach interested. I communicate throughout the season. Sometimes, helping an athlete find a college is more fun than the race itself.

Evaluating Yourself As A Coach

When I reflect as a coach, I want to be excellent. It doesn't come overnight and it's not easy. I fail at times, but I constantly reflect on what I could do better. I reach out to other coaches, mentors, and communicate with my assistants and runners. I want my kids to be the best runner they can be and the best person. When I think about what makes an excellent coach, I came down to these ideas:

- Do not be arrogant and have confidence. Developing a swagger and believing in yourself is not the same as being arrogant. Help the kids learn this.

- Making a runner mentally tough is harder than making them physically strong.

- Wishes do not exist, only hard work, heart, and support

- If you want to be perfect, practice that way.

- Racing has to be broken down into parts and practiced to become better

- Don't train to train, train for a purpose

- Give everything at the end of the race; find a new maximum to conquer

- Run fast in practice; running slow distance creates slow runners

- Conduct one full speed workout at least once a week, and supplement speed across each day (2x300s to practice finishing)

- Your athletes know their bodies better than you. If they doubt they can run, don't pressure them into it.

- Running too many races is foolish. Your body can only take so much.

- Remaining aware during the race allows you to make better decisions.

- Winning isn't everything; find success in all times.

- Most important, have a life outside of the sport. If this consumes your mind, you will burn out.

Evaluating Your Program

A coach's season doesn't end with a last meet, but with a cooling period. That's when you take the time to review what you accomplished at the end of your season. The sooner you do this, the easier it is to remember. What went right, what went wrong, and what you can do to be better next year.

To be quite frank, if you had a successful year, do not make a lot of changes. If it's not broke, don't fix it. However, every program needs fine tuning. We want to evolve. Nothing 5-10 years ago still fully works. Times change, and you need to be open to making changes as the years turn.

What Does Success Look Like?

Your picture of success is entirely up to you. It's based on your program's history and expectations. When I took over, we didn't have a program. We didn't have expectations, so I changed the culture. Our vision of success is making winning a couple of invites, placing high at conference, making the Sectional at state as a team, and everyone finishing with at least one PR.

We also set personal and team goals and we evaluate those goals as the season goes on. If the kids meet their personal and team goals, I would call that a success. The only way the team can "fail" is if they don't live up to their potential. What is that potential in your eyes, and your team's eyes?

Evaluating The Season

I'm not going to lie. When the season is over, there is a sense of relief. The final two weeks always feel like a grind, but we preach to finish strong. We do not want to take our foot off the gas until the season is done. When the season concludes, we can finally relax. A break is necessary for everyone, even the coach.

After you take your break, which is likely a month or two, given if you help out with track or not, you should feel some excitement about the next season. Look back on the season and make fine tunes for your next season. If that is track season for you, it's devoting your time towards the same amount of runners again.

When looking back at your season, try to correct the mistakes. We all make mistakes. It's natural, but don't make revolutionary changes to your program. Make the small adjustments. Again, we want to evolve over time.

Evaluating Your Future

The only time I think you should be worried is if you are not excited about next season. If you feel that the next season is just going to be a grind, you are doing everyone a disservice. There is a life outside of coaching. I always thought that if I leave my program, I want it to be in better shape than it was left off for me.

The offseason is a good time to reflect on the good and the bad. It's important to take one year at a time. I always thought I would coach three sports my whole life. Then, I got married and had my daughter. For now, the compromise is two sports. My point is that you cannot predict the future. You can only take it one day at a time. In our case, only one season at a time.

Conclusion

Being a cross country coach is so rewarding. Being able to help mold young men and women into better athletes is a dream job. It takes a lot of work and there are likely tips that weren't ever mentioned in this book. Just remember to do your best and take pride in being a coach.

About the Expert

Kyle Daubs is a 2011 graduate of Charleston High School and a 2015 graduate of Eastern Illinois University. He received his degree in special education. He has taught special education the last four years. During this time, he started the cross country cooperative for Lowpoint-Washburn-Roanoke-Benson in 2016. During his time, he guided the girls cross country team to a conference championship in his second year of coaching and took the team to the IHSA Sectional meet.

He has also coached track since 2015. Since 2015, he has sent 22 athletes to state competition, including coaching three all-state relays and three all-state individuals. His wife, Jordan, and him live in Roanoke where they have a daughter, Penelope.

HowExpert publishes quick 'how to' guides on all topics from A to Z by everyday experts. Visit HowExpert.com to learn more.

Recommended Resources

- HowExpert.com – Quick 'How To' Guides on All Topics from A to Z by Everyday Experts.
- HowExpert.com/free – Free HowExpert Email Newsletter.
- HowExpert.com/books – HowExpert Books
- HowExpert.com/courses – HowExpert Courses
- HowExpert.com/clothing – HowExpert Clothing
- HowExpert.com/membership – HowExpert Membership Site
- HowExpert.com/affiliates – HowExpert Affiliate Program
- HowExpert.com/writers – Write About Your #1 Passion/Knowledge/Expertise & Become a HowExpert Author.
- HowExpert.com/resources – Additional HowExpert Recommended Resources
- YouTube.com/HowExpert – Subscribe to HowExpert YouTube.
- Instagram.com/HowExpert – Follow HowExpert on Instagram.
- Facebook.com/HowExpert – Follow HowExpert on Facebook.

Made in the USA
Monee, IL
06 August 2023

40514091R00059